SOLUTIONS TO MARRIAGE PROBLEM:

Discover The Seven Principles On How To Make Marriage Work Smoothly

Rosemerie Richardson

Table of contents

to the area of the brain where it stores "all the crucial knowledge about your partner's life."

Knowing Your Spouse:

Healthy spouses have left enough

place in their brains known for their marriage. The significant events in their past are crucial and they continue to add to their memory the facts and emotions of their spouse's world moving ahead. When he requests a coffee from Starbucks, she already knows the sort of espresso he prefers. If she leaves on a business trip, he knows what TV programs to record so she may watch upon her return.

Deeper Intimacy And Connection:

Knowing the other spouse creates a stronger connection and intimacy in the marriage. They will know one other's faith, life objectives, concerns, and hopes for the future, knowing your spouse and vice versa deepens the love each has for the other. Without such a love map, a couple cannot fully know one another.

Love Map And Commitment:

Without knowing the other, there is no meaningful closeness. Healthy marriages begin with knowing, then knowing leads to trust, which leads to taking larger chances, and greater risks lead to a stronger commitment. Unhealthy marriages somehow lose touch and verify why many couples state the grounds for their divorce were due to “growing apart

OVERCOME GRIDLOCK:

Have you ever found yourself at a point in your marriage when you and your spouse disagree and it feels like there is no way forward? At some point, in any marriage, this is a possibility. It happens when you can't learn to live with your perpetual problems. Every couple has two kinds of problems; perpetual (70%) and solvable (30%). How a couple handles the perpetual problems is critical to avoiding gridlock.

Here are some possible issues that can be the source of gridlock:

- She wants another child, he doesn't

- He wants to adopt, but she doesn't
- She wants to attend this church, he wants to attend another
- He wants to go out and enjoy friends, she would rather stay at home
- She doesn't mind clutter, he can't stand the sight of dust
- He wants a dog, she wants a cat
- She wants him to lead family devotions, he wants her to
- He wants a mini-SUV, and she wants a mini-van
- She wants to decorate the house, he wants to increase their giving to charity
- He hates being late, she doesn't mind being late

If you take a thorough look at the numerous sorts of challenges that might lead to congestion, you will find that it can be anything! It might be anything as big as having children or a spiritual belief to something as trivial as how neat and organized you desire your home to be. Whether they appear serious or small to outsiders, all gridlocked conflicts have four features. You'll know you've hit congestion if:

1. You've had the same debate again and again with no resolution.
2. Neither of you can approach the matter with comedy, empathy, or compassion.

3. The subject is growing more contentious as time goes on.
4. Compromise feels hard because it would entail selling out–giving up something crucial and fundamental to your views, values, or sense of self.

Does it sound familiar? Do you and your spouse or another couple you know to describe a difficulty in their marriage in this way? If so, what can you do? Here are four things. stalemate indicates that there are basic principles and beliefs behind the impasse. So although the problem may appear simple on the surface, there is much more going on below.

To navigate your way out of congestion, you have to first grasp that no matter how trivial the problem, deadlock is an indication that you both have ambitions for your life that the other isn't aware of, hasn't acknowledged, or doesn't respect.

By dreams I mean the ambitions, aspirations, and desires that are part of your identity and provide purpose and meaning to your life To prevent gridlock, you must become aware of the dreams that lie behind the disagreement, begin to appreciate your spouse's aspirations and learn to integrate their dreams into the relationship. When you have reached an impasse, there is a loss of respect, liking, and adoration. You must regain that. The way you accomplish it is by asking your spouse what the area of blockage means to them. What dream is it linked to

CREATE SHARED MEANING:

As you listen, you may begin to see the deeper logic and start to reconnect with your spouse. This may seem simplistic, but it isn't. It is never simple to make attempts to understand your spouse and listen to them as they share their deeper dreams and aspirations.

Throughout this blog series, we have been reviewing the principles that make marriage work as theorized. If you have accomplished the first six principles, more than likely you have a happy and stable marriage. As a reminder, those first six principles are: Building Love Maps, Nurturing Your

Fondness and Admiration, Turning Toward Your Partner, Let Your Partner Influence You, Solving Your Solvable Problems, and Overcoming Gridlock. The final principle in the series is Creating Shared Meaning. This involves both partners meshing together their life philosophies and honoring each other's dreams.

Gottman states, "The more you can agree about the fundamentals of life, the richer, more profound, and in a sense, easier your marriage is likely to be." To encourage honesty within your relationship, there must be a welcoming atmosphere. Do you think you are open to your partner's perspective? Exploring deeper meaning within your relationship is a lifelong process. As you and your partner grow and change, so will your values and goals. The key is to be open to your partner's beliefs so that the two of you can create a joyful life together.

As we wrap up this series, I hope you have taken away some new knowledge and tools that can apply to your relationship. Every day you can build the change you want to see in your marriage. Just remember, "No book or therapist can solve all of your marital problems. But learning the Seven Principles really can change the course of your relationship.

KINDS OF MATERIAL CONFLICT:

In marriage, conflict occurs when the needs and desires of spouses diverge and are thus incompatible. Because spouses interact with each other regarding several issues important to their marriage over time, the conflict will inevitably occur to at least some degree in every marriage. It is not the existence of conflict in marriage per se that is detrimental to marital satisfaction or stability, but how spouses manage conflict when it occurs.

Conflicts can be settled positively through discussion, but in some cases may result in the escalation of arguing without resolution, or with each spouse ignoring the area of conflict in an attempt to prevent negative marital interactions. The quality of the marriage suffers when conflicts remain unresolved, and in some marriages, the inability to successfully manage conflict can lead to physical abuse, sometimes with severe consequences. Understanding the causes and consequences of marital conflict has been the target of a growing body of empirical research, and the results of this research have been useful in developing therapeutic programs aimed at assisting spouses to manage conflict positively.

When faced with marital conflict, certain people are more likely than others to engage in negative interpersonal behaviors. For instance, some people tend to be very anxious about how much their romantic partners love them, fearing that their partners may eventually abandon the relationship. When relationship conflicts occur, these anxious individuals are more likely to become very upset and believe that their partners will leave them.

Sooner or later, every married couple fights. However, some conflicts are guaranteed to come up between spouses at some point in your relationship. In our experience, the top 5 conflicts every married couple faces are incredibly common and can cause a lot of tension in relationships when left unresolved. Wondering what those common conflicts are? Let's dive right in.

1. FINANCES

Money is one of the most prevalent concerns married couples quarrel over. Whether you're talking about spending preferences, how much is in your savings account, how much you should spend on trips and holidays, or simply how the two of you perceive finances, money is a heated issue. However, it's also a subject many couples avoid because it is so combustible.

2. INTIMACY

Sex is yet another prevalent argument between couples. Like money, it's a very sensitive issue and may leave both husband and wife feeling vulnerable and sad. Differing intimacy demands, frequency of sex, and conveying individual wishes may all influence issues focused around the bedroom.

3. CAREERS

Work is a hot-button subject in many couples because it can create such an imbalance in your life if you're not watchful. Creating a work-life balance that works for your family is crucial, otherwise, it will be difficult to dedicate the time to your marriage and your family that you'd want to. Couples may quarrel over working too much or too little, and about how each spouse will leverage their jobs to provide for the family and prepare for the future.

4. KIDS

Parenting issues are tricky to handle. Spouses sometimes dispute over how to discipline their kids, what limits to establish, and how to go about carving out time for their marriage in the middle of hectic child-rearing seasons (particularly while young children are still in the house) (especially when small children are still in the home). The attitudes, unstated standards, and expectations we establish in our early family experiences also affect our parenting as adults, and frequently figure into parental problems.

5. CHORES\scommonly argue over home duties. Fights may come from fundamental views about how duties relate to

conventional gender roles, expectations from the families we grew up in, and personal preferences about responsibilities in the family. When we married and build our own new home, it's up to us to put our heads together and develop something that's completely our own. Unfortunately, the procedure isn't always easy or simple.

TURN TOWARD EACH OTHER:

It's your wedding day. The universe begins a huge egg timer set for six years. When the egg timer goes off, you'll either be divorced or you won't. You've heard the notion that 50% of marriages end in divorce, but someone knows certain methods that may enhance your prospects of making it. More crucially, they knew of a specific approach that would practically assure that you would divorce before the timer went out. Would you want to know it?

Of course, you would. You would do everything it takes to guarantee that you safeguarded yourself from divorce. It's no mystery, and chances are, it's right in front of you. Many of the couples stayed together. Many divorced. The couples who remained married were substantially better at one thing: the third level of the Sound Relationship House, Turn Towards Instead of Away. At the six-year follow-up, couples who remained married turned towards one another 86% of the time.

Couples that divorced averaged just 33% of the time. This is a pretty incredible piece of data. It suggests that there is something you can do today that will dramatically change the course of your relationship. More importantly, it suggests that there is something that you cannot do that will lead to its demise. So, how do you turn towards instead of away? To understand turning, you have to first understand bids. Turn towards what? Bids for connection

A bid is any attempt from one partner to another for attention, affirmation, affection, or any other positive connection. Bids show up in simple ways, a smile or wink, and in more complex ways, like a request for advice or help. In general, women make more bids than men, but in the healthiest relationships, both partners are comfortable making all kinds of bids.

As you continue moving through life together, you will undoubtedly have to risk heading into more vulnerable territory. This will be easier if you've committed to building a solid friendship based on Building Love Maps, Sharing Fondness and Admiration, and Turning Towards Instead of Away.

NATURE YOUR FONDNESS AND ADMIRATION:

No one's perfect, including you and the person you're married to. Maybe she squeezes the toothpaste from the middle or he leaves the toilet seat up. Maybe she is bull-headed and he is annoyingly indecisive. Maybe one of you is a workaholic and another spends too much money.

Despite these flaws, it's likely that deep down you believe your spouse is a good person who is worthy of honor and respect. At the heart of nearly every marriage lies this fundamental belief: that one's partner in marriage is a respectable, likable person.

it calls the "fondness and admiration system." People who are happily married like each other. This probably sounds like an obvious, overly simplistic concept. But it's overlooked more often than people think. Why is it important? couples who nurture their fondness and admiration for one another are better able to accept each other's flaws and weaknesses and prevent them from threatening their relationship.

Fondness and admiration protect against feeling contempt for your spouse, a dangerous emotion that too many partners develop toward one another as the years go by. Feelings of contempt can quickly break down the bonds of friendship between husband and wife. Here are ideas to help you revive and nurture your fondness and admiration for each other:

List each other's positive qualities. List as many things as you can think of. (Is he or she intelligent, witty, organized, creative, attractive, or relaxed?) For each quality you list, think of a specific incident when your spouse displayed that quality. Write it down. Share your lists.

Many couples rekindled their fondness and admiration by recalling happy events of their past 94% of couples who have positive memories of their history together are likely to have a happy future.
How did you meet? What were your first impressions of each other?

What do you remember about the time you were dating? What were your favorite things to do or places to go together?

How did you decide to get married? How did you know your spouse was the person you wanted to spend the rest of your life with? Was it an easy or hard decision?

What do you remember about your wedding? Your honeymoon?

How was your first year of marriage? What things did you have to adjust to as newlyweds?

Looking back, what moments stand out as the happiest times in your marriage?

What moments stand out as difficult times in your marriage? How did you get through those hard times? Why did you stay together despite them?

They Answer the following questions together, (If it would help, invite a close friend or family member to act as the interviewer and ask you the questions.)1

Practice positive thinking. Thinking positively might seem simplistic, but researchers have found it to be a powerful tool for overcoming depression. Found it equally useful for overcoming negativity and hopelessness in troubled marriages. Some ideas about how to think positively about your marriage include:

Each day when you wake up, think of one positive thought about your spouse, such as a trait you admire, a talent, something you especially like about him or her, a feature of your relationship that you like, etc. If this is difficult, try thinking of something positive your spouse has done. Write down your thought on a piece of paper. Put it in a place where you'll see it and think of it during the day, such as in your pocket, on your car dashboard, or your desk.

During the day, especially when you and your spouse are apart, repeat the thought silently to yourself.

Do this with a different thought at least five days a week for at least two weeks.

As you rehearse positive thoughts about your spouse, positive feelings about him or she will begin to come more naturally. It will be easier to see the good things in your marriage.

PATNER INFLUENCE:

Ways to Positively Influence Your Spouse\sRespect. Be polite. Acknowledge and be proactive in appreciating strengths. You may affect your spouse's self image in a favorable manner with an attitude of respect. You may influence others' conduct and opinion of your spouse by your respect of her/him.

Helpfulness. Feeling like you are supported by your partner might make a great influence. Sometimes the aid comes in the form of really doing something, and other times it's just via your presence. Your spouse will feel better about the result of any circumstance if they're safe in the understanding you are on their side.

Attentiveness. Your quick attention may impact a result. In our culture we're absorbed by digital gadgets. Try something new: drop the digital gadgets at the door, and concentrate on your partner. Your capacity to affect your marriage will sky-rocket when your focus is on your relationship – not outside of it...

Influence means a power to affect persons or events; determine and shape events and outcomes.

Use your influence for good.

Have you examined how your conduct is impacting your spouse? And your lives together? Give it some thought.

www.ingramcontent.com/pod-product-compliance
Lightning Source LLC
LaVergne TN
LVHW020537160826
845677LV00015B/4109

* 9 7 9 8 8 4 8 1 4 4 7 9 6 *